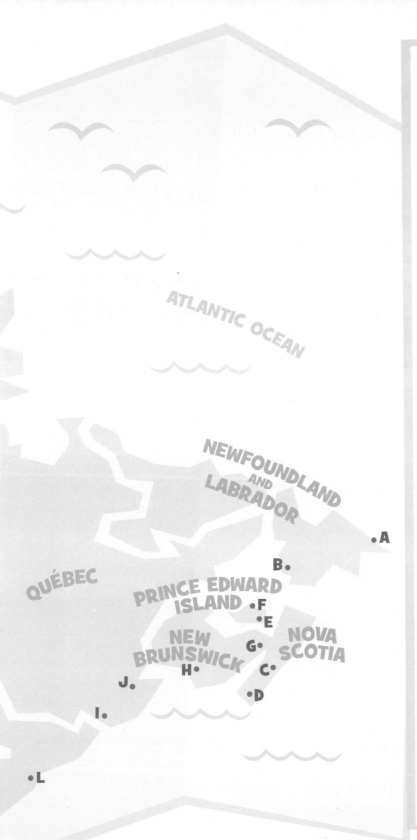

What did Sophie and Bear see in...

...Newfoundland and Labrador?

A: The Cape Spear Lighthouse. It's the oldest lighthouse in Newfoundland.

B: Beluga whales, which often swim in the waters around this province.

...Nova Scotia?

C: Nova Scotian seafood in a yummy chowder.

D: A duck-tolling retriever. That's the official dog of Nova Scotia.

...Prince Edward Island?

E: The world-famous red clay soil beaches of P.E.I.

F: Fishermen. That's one of the province's main jobs.

...New Brunswick?

G: The Hopewell Rocks, or Flowerpot Rocks, in the Bay of Fundy.

H: The Hartland Bridge. It's the world's longest covered bridge.

...Québec?

I: Montréal's beautiful church, the Notre-Dame Basilica.

J: Jugglers who perform in the older parts of Montréal and Québec City.

...Ontario?

K: A black bear eating wild Ontario berries.

L: A ferry sailing between Toronto Harbour and the Toronto Islands.

...Manitoba?

M: The Mounties, or Royal Canadian Mounted Police, who protect people across Canada.

N: The Royal Canadian Mint in Winnipeg, where Canadian coins are made.

...Nunavut?

O: A snowy owl, which lives in Nunavut all year round.

P: A polar bear, the largest land carnivore in the world.

...Northwest Territories?

Q: An inuksuk. It's a large stone structure built by the Inuit to mark places and guide travellers.

R: The Mackenzie River, which is the longest river in Canada.

...Saskatchewan?

S: The University Bridge in Saskatoon. It crosses the South Saskatchewan River.

T: A train carrying wheat grown by prairie farmers to cities across Canada.

...Alberta?

U: Canada Olympic Park in Calgary. It was built for the 1988 Winter Olympics.

V: Drumheller, Alberta. It's world-famous for its dinosaur fossils.

...Yukon?

W: A tundra moose, the world's largest moose.

X: A gold nugget! Back in 1897, Dawson City, Yukon was where the Klondike Gold Rush happened.

...British Columbia?

Y and **Z**: The Strait of Georgia. This big body of water sits between Vancouver Island and Vancouver.

Where are you Bear?

A Canadian Alphabet Adventure

Written by Frieda Wishinsky • *Illustrated by Sean L. Moore*

Owl kids

Owlkids Books Inc.
10 Lower Spadina Avenue, Suite 400, Toronto, Ontario M5V 2Z2
www.owlkids.com

Distributed in Canada by Raincoast Books
9050 Shaughnessy Street, Vancouver, British Columbia V6P 6E5

Distributed in the United States by Publishers Group West
1700 Fourth Street, Berkeley, California 94710

With thanks to Sheba, Mary Beth, Anne, John, Barb, and Sean. You made it fun! — F.W.

For My Aunt Elaine. Mother, Sister, Wife, and Teacher. — S.L.M.

Library and Archives Canada Cataloguing in Publication

Wishinsky, Frieda
        Where are you, Bear? : a Canadian alphabet adventure / Frieda
Wishinsky ; illustrated by Sean L. Moore.

ISBN 978-1-897349-91-5

        1. Canada--Pictorial works--Juvenile literature. 2. English
language--Alphabet--Juvenile literature. 3. Alphabet books.
I. Moore, Sean, 1976- II. Title.

FC58.W58 2010   j971   C2010-900618-6

Library of Congress Control Number: 2010920583

Design: Barb Kelly

 Canada Council   Conseil des Arts
for the Arts   du Canada

 ONTARIO ARTS COUNCIL
CONSEIL DES ARTS DE L'ONTARIO

We acknowledge the financial support of the Canada Council for the Arts, the Ontario Arts Council, the Government of Canada through the Book Publishing Industry Development Program (BPIDP), and the Government of Ontario through the Ontario Media Development Corporation's Book Initiative for our publishing activities.

Printed by WKT Co. Ltd.
Printed in Shenzhen, Guangdong, China March/2010
Job #09CB4074

A   B   C   D   E   F

Publisher of Chirp, chickaDEE and OWL
www.owlkids.com

Sophie couldn't wait!
Soon, she and Bear would visit Grandma in Vancouver.

"Time to go, Sophie!"

"But I can't find Bear."

"Where are you, Bear?
I have to go. I'll miss you!

We would have had
so much fun!"

"Oh no! Sophie! I'm coming, I'll find you."

Aa Adventure

Newfoundland and Labrador

"What a big adventure!"

Bb

Beluga whale

"What big bubbles!"

Cc Chowder

"Let's eat."

Dd
Dog

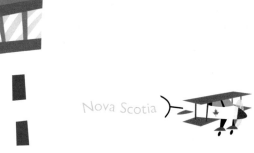

"Let go!"

Ee Earth

Ff
Fish

"Uh-oh. Stuck."

Gg Goose

"Yuck! Poo!"

New Brunswick

Hh
Harbour

"Sea goo!"

Ii Île de Montréal

Québec

"Je suis heureuse." (I am happy.)

Jj

Jugglers

"Je ne suis pas heureux." (I am not happy.)

Kk Kayak

"*Wild bear!*"

Ll
Lake

Ontario

"Wild ride!"

Mm Mounties

"One. Two."

Nn
Nickel

"One. Two."

Oo Owl

"Hoot!"

Pp

Polar bear

"Scoot!"

Qq Quiet

Northwest Territories

"Not a sound."

Rr
River

"Not so fast!"

Ss Sunset

"Wow! Red sky!"

Tt

Train

"Wow! Red train!"

Uu Up

"Hello up there!"

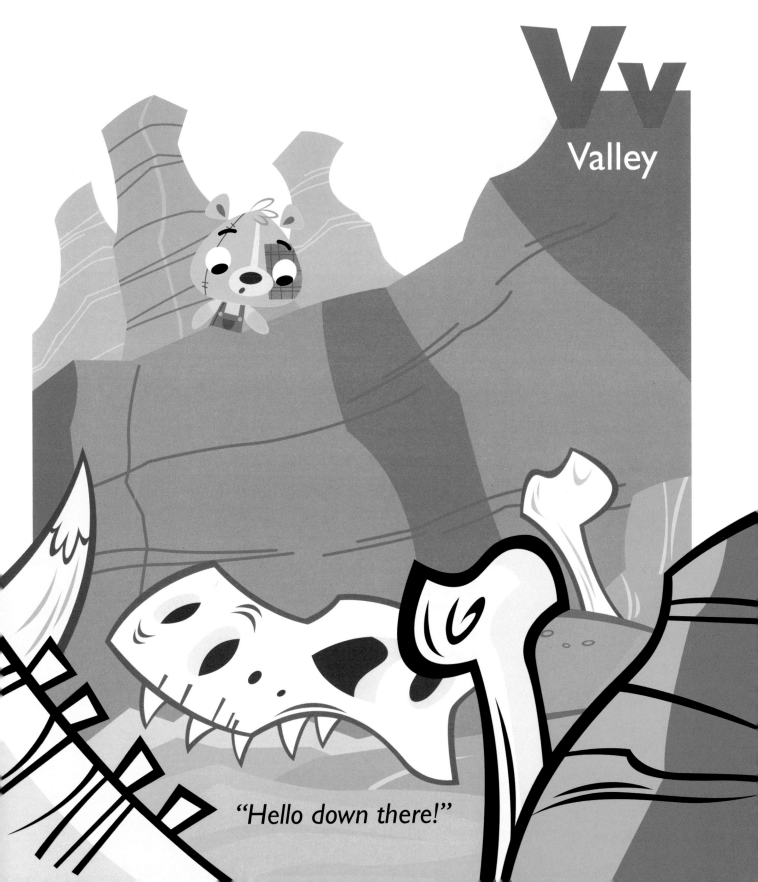

Ww Woods

Yukon

"Look what I see!"

Xx

X marks the spot

"Look what I found!"

Yy Yacht

"Bear!"

Zz
Zoom

"Sophie!"

"Where were you, Bear?"

What did Sophie and Bear see in...

...Newfoundland and Labrador?
A: The Cape Spear Lighthouse. It's the oldest lighthouse in Newfoundland.
B: Beluga whales, which often swim in the waters around this province.

...Nova Scotia?
C: Nova Scotian seafood in a yummy chowder.
D: A duck-tolling retriever. That's the official dog of Nova Scotia.

...Prince Edward Island?
E: The world-famous red clay soil beaches of P.E.I.
F: Fishermen. That's one of the province's main jobs.

...New Brunswick?
G: The Hopewell Rocks, or Flowerpot Rocks, in the Bay of Fundy.
H: The Hartland Bridge. It's the world's longest covered bridge.

...Québec?
I: Montréal's beautiful church, the Notre-Dame Basilica.
J: Jugglers who perform in the older parts of Montréal and Québec City.

...Ontario?
K: A black bear eating wild Ontario berries.
L: A ferry sailing between Toronto Harbour and the Toronto Islands.

...Manitoba?
M: The Mounties, or Royal Canadian Mounted Police, who protect people across Canada.
N: The Royal Canadian Mint in Winnipeg, where Canadian coins are made.

...Nunavut?
O: A snowy owl, which lives in Nunavut all year round.
P: A polar bear, the largest land carnivore in the world.

...Northwest Territories?
Q: An inuksuk. It's a large stone structure built by the Inuit to mark places and guide travellers.
R: The Mackenzie River, which is the longest river in Canada.

...Saskatchewan?
S: The University Bridge in Saskatoon. It crosses the South Saskatchewan River.
T: A train carrying wheat grown by prairie farmers to cities across Canada.

...Alberta?
U: Canada Olympic Park in Calgary. It was built for the 1988 Winter Olympics.
V: Drumheller, Alberta. It's world-famous for its dinosaur fossils.

...Yukon?
W: A tundra moose, the world's largest moose.
X: A gold nugget! Back in 1897, Dawson City, Yukon was where the Klondike Gold Rush happened.

...British Columbia?
Y and **Z**: The Strait of Georgia. This big body of water sits between Vancouver Island and Vancouver.

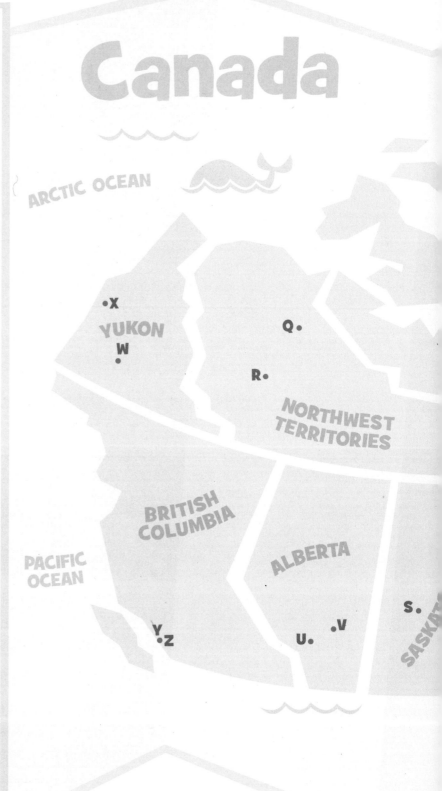